The Effects of
Recent Tax Reforms
on Labor Supply

The Effects of Recent Tax Reforms on Labor Supply

Thomas J. Kniesner and
James P. Ziliak

The AEI Press

Publisher for the American Enterprise Institute
WASHINGTON, D.C.
1998

We appreciate the financial support of the Office of the Vice President for Research and the University Graduate School of Indiana University; the Hoover Institution of Stanford University; the Department of Economics of University College, London; the Center for Economic Research of Tilburg University; and the Center for Risk Analysis of Harvard University.

Available in the United States from the AEI Press, c/o Publisher Resources Inc., 1224 Heil Quaker Blvd., P.O. Box 7001, La Vergne, TN 37086-7001. To order, call: 1-800-269-6267. Distributed outside the United States by arrangement with Eurospan, 3 Henrietta Street, London WC2E 8LU England.

ISBN 0-8447-7087-6

1 3 5 7 9 10 8 6 4 2

THE AEI PRESS
Publisher for the American Enterprise Institute
1150 17th Street, N.W., Washington, D.C. 20036

Printed in the United States of America

Contents

Foreword

Economists, policy makers, and business executives are keenly interested in fundamental tax reform. High marginal tax rates, complex tax provisions, disincentives for saving and investment, and solvency problems in the social security program provide reasons to contemplate how reforms of the tax code and other public policies toward saving and investment might increase economic efficiency, simplify the tax code, and enhance fairness. Many economists believe that gains to the economy from an overhaul of the income tax or from a move to a broad-based consumption tax can be measured in the trillions of dollars. Most conventional economic models indicate a potential for large gains from tax reform.

While many economists agree broadly on the simple analytics of tax reform, they are in much less agreement on such key empirical questions as how much saving or investment would rise in response to a switch to a consumption tax, how much capital accumulation would increase under a partial privatization of social security, how reform would affect the distribution of taxes, and how international capital markets influence the effects of tax reforms in the United States. This lack of professional consensus has made the policy debate fuzzy and confusing.

With these concerns in mind, Diana Furchtgott-Roth and I organized a tax reform seminar series at the

American Enterprise Institute beginning in January 1996. At each seminar, an economist presented new empirical research on topics relating to fundamental tax reform. These topics include transition problems in moving to a consumption tax, the effect of taxation on household saving, distributional effects of consumption taxes in the long and short run, issues in the taxation of financial services, privatizing social security as a fundamental tax reform, international issues in consumption taxation, distributional consequences of reductions in the capital gains tax, effects of tax reform on pension saving and nonpension saving, effects of tax reform on labor supply, consequences of tax reform on business investment, and likely prototypes for fundamental tax reform.

The goal of the pamphlet series in fundamental tax reform is to distribute research on economic issues in tax reform to a broad audience. Each study in the series reflects many insightful comments by seminar participants—economists, attorneys, accountants, and journalists in the tax policy community. Diana and I are especially grateful to the two discussants of each paper, who offered the perspectives of an economist and an attorney.

I would like to thank the American Enterprise Institute for providing financial support for the seminar series and pamphlet series.

R. GLENN HUBBARD
Columbia University

1
Introduction

Although research on labor supply acknowledges the work-incentive effects of income taxes, a shortcoming in the empirical literature is an inattention to the lifetime effects of multiple income taxes. Adding the taxation of capital income to the taxation of earned income complicates empirical research because dual progressive taxation generates multiyear links in disposable incomes. We studied the labor market behavior of prime-aged married men for a decade to understand their short-run and long-run work preferences. In our research, we wanted to determine how progressive taxation of both wage and capital incomes affects the lifetime supply of labor.

A regularly appearing result in past empirical research on men's labor supply, whether it acknowledges or ignores income taxation, is that wage effects are small and statistically fragile. Many empirical results are at odds with how the prototypical economically rational worker would behave. To elaborate, suppose a researcher finds that higher wages make men want to work more. Moving to a less graduated or flatter income tax then induces more hours worked and reduces the economic burden of the income tax, which is the well-being a worker loses under income taxation compared with paying an equivalent tax bill generated without regard to income. Alternatively, if we find that higher wages make people want to work less, then the economic implications of a flatter income tax contradict many of the usual arguments used by proponents of tax reform. The lack of consensus on the magnitude and sign of the effects of wages on the labor supply continues to muddy discussions of the welfare implications of a flatter tax structure.

Our research produces improved estimates of how progressive income taxation affects workers' incentives to stay in the labor force throughout their lifetime. For tractability, we summarize the link between work and disposable income as a smoothly curved line, which mitigates the statistical problems from incorrectly imputing a marginal tax rate. Incorrectly assigning a worker's tax bracket is likely because most surveys do not provide detailed information on deductions and sources of income. Our statistical procedure first examines short-run wage effects on labor supply in light of the worker's asset holdings, which reveals short-run preferences toward work. We then examine changes in wealth throughout the lifetime and long-run fluctuations in labor supply to infer long-run preferences toward work.

We find a number of noteworthy results. Using the most accurate measure of the rate of pay matters to the estimates. Evidence of multiyear links in disposable incomes supports our statistical approach. Our results indicate the need to use longitudinal information on individuals and to incorporate the joint progressive taxation of wage and capital incomes in research on labor supply. On average, we find that a 10 percent reduction in the marginal tax rate increases the labor supplied by prime-aged men by about 0.6 percent. The effect on tax rates varies across wealth groups such that the wealthiest 25 percent of prime-aged married working men is 40 percent more responsive to tax rate changes than the poorest 25 percent. Our calculations indicate that although recent U.S. tax reforms were revenue reducing, they stimulated the labor supplied by males by about 3 percent and lowered the economic burden from a progressive income tax by about 16 percent.

2
Tax Reform in the 1980s— Controversy and Consensus

Establishing the amount to which income taxes change the supply of labor is a central issue in discussions of tax reform. Because income taxation produces about three-fourths of federal revenues, for example, accurate predictions of labor supply responses are crucial to accurate predictions of the budgetary consequences of tax reforms. There has been significant disagreement over the size of the work disincentive effects of income taxation in the U.S. male labor force. The empirical research on labor supply of the 1970s, as surveyed in Pencavel (1986), indicates that changes in the after-tax wage do not produce changes in the supply of men's labor. Compared with the research of the 1970s, the research in the 1980s, as surveyed in Hausman (1985), indicates a larger behavioral response and attendant welfare loss from progressive income taxes.

The debate over the labor market consequences of tax reform is illustrated particularly well in a recent dialogue between the U.S. Treasury and a former chairman of the President's Council of Economic Advisers, Martin Feldstein. In 1993 the Clinton administration proposed a 30 percent increase in marginal tax rates for the highest-income Americans with the accompanying belief that labor supply outcomes would be largely unchanged so that revenue collections would also rise by about 30 percent. Feldstein (1993) contended that revenues would rise by much less than 30 percent, maybe even fall, because not only would the tax increase make primary workers reduce their hours worked but it would also make some secondary workers leave the labor force.

The issue of the labor market disincentive effects of income taxation is now at the core of the dual discussions of the desirability of a balanced-budget amendment to the Constitution and a proportional income tax. To explain, suppose the typical worker has a lower marginal tax rate under a single-rate or so-called flat tax system than under our current progressive tax system. If labor supply does not respond much to the higher after-tax wage, then tax collections will fall, and the flat tax will enlarge any existing budget shortfalls. Alternatively, if when confronted with the lower tax rate under the flat tax the typical worker increases hours worked, then tax collections will not fall proportionately as much as the tax rate and could even rise.

Hours, Wages, and Tax Burdens

To set the stage for our empirical research to come, we now examine how hours of work, wages, and the average tax burdens of prime-aged married men evolved over the 1980s. The two major tax reforms of the 1980s are the Economic Recovery Tax Act (ERTA) of 1981 and the Tax Reform Act of 1986 (TRA86). ERTA reduced marginal tax rates by 23 percent on average within each bracket. TRA86 reduced the number of tax brackets from fourteen to four and introduced base-broadening measures such as eliminating the preferential treatment of capital gains. The top marginal tax rate dropped from 70 percent in 1981 to 50 percent in 1982, then dropped further to 28 percent in 1987, while the average federal tax rate fell by 25 percent during the 1980s. The data we will use for our summary examination of the temporal patterns of tax reforms, work hours, wages, and average tax rates are from the Panel Study of Income Dynamics for 1978–1987, which is described in more detail in chapter 5.

Figure 2–1 depicts how average annual hours of work remained fairly stable over the period as a whole, rising only about 1 percent. Average annual hours worked fell by about 4 percent from 1978 to 1982 but rose by about 5 percent during 1982 to 1987. Figure 2–2 confirms the well-known stagnation of the average real gross wage during the 1980s, although the real wage did rise as much as 3 percent after the 1986 tax reform. A more meaningful upward movement happened in the average real after-tax wage. From 1978 to 1981, net wages declined steadily by about 10 percent, then rose about 6 percent from 1981 to 1984, held steady between 1984 and 1986, and finally rose about 10 percent in the year following TRA86. The fact that average annual hours worked fell in 1982, even though the average net wage rose, underscores the depth of the 1982 recession. Clearly, the deep recession of 1981–1982 could confound any test of the labor supply effects of tax reform, so our statistical model must account for the influence of the business cycle on labor supply.

Figures 2–3 and 2–4 depict average marginal tax rates and average tax rates. Each diagram contains two rates. The lower rate accounts for federal income taxation only, and the upper rate appends the contribution of the payroll tax rate and the worker's state-specific average income tax rate. We include payroll and state income tax rates to highlight their offsetting effect on federal tax reform and to get a better description of the total tax burden confronting the typical worker. As

FIGURE 2–1
AVERAGE ANNUAL HOURS OF WORK FOR PRIME-AGED
MARRIED MEN, 1978–1987

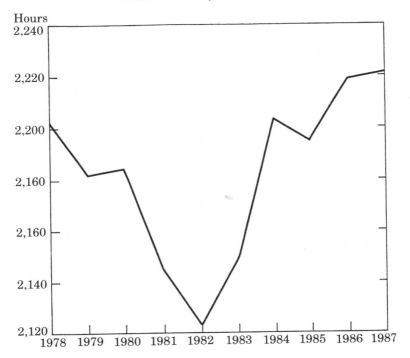

SOURCE: Panel Study of Income Dynamics.

shown in figure 2–3, federal marginal tax rates for the average worker fell nearly 12 percent from 1981 to 1983 and fell nearly 14 percent from 1986 to 1987. Total marginal tax rates fell less, 8 percent during 1981–1983 and 11 percent during 1986–1987. A similar pattern of dual declines in the early and middle 1980s holds for the average federal and average total tax rates shown in figure 2–4.

To gauge the distributional consequences of the tax reforms, in figures 2–5 and 2–6 we disaggregate the average federal and total tax rates by gross income

FIGURE 2–2
AVERAGE GROSS AND NET WAGE OF PRIME-AGED
MARRIED MEN, 1978–1987

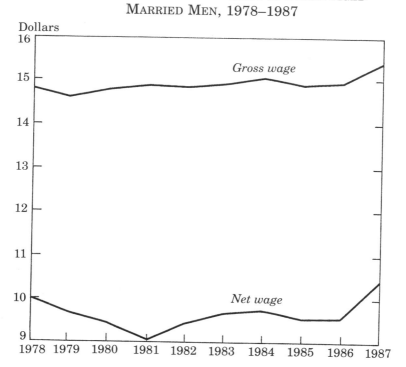

SOURCE: Panel Study of Income Dynamics.

deciles in the first years following the tax reforms, 1978, 1982, and 1987. In 1977 President Carter approved a mild reform, the Tax Reduction and Simplification Act of 1977, which provides a benchmark for the reforms of the 1980s. The primary feature of the Carter administration reform for individual income taxes was the replacement of the standard deduction with a so-called zero bracket amount, which resulted in a 15 percent increase in the amount of excluded income for taxpayers choosing not to itemize. Figures 2–5 and 2–6 show that TRA86 was the most generous to all taxpayers,

FIGURE 2–3
AVERAGE MARGINAL TAX RATES FOR PRIME-AGED
MARRIED MEN, 1978–1987

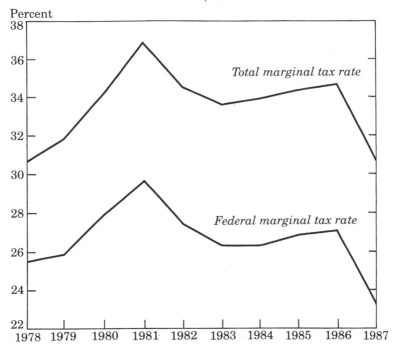

SOURCE: Panel Study of Income Dynamics.

although we note that average burdens were higher in 1982 than in 1978. The higher average tax rates in 1982 reflect the so-called bracket creep in federal tax rates during the high inflation years of 1980 and 1981 and the 15 percent increase in the payroll tax rate from 5.85 percent to 6.70 percent. The overall tax burden, as measured by the average total tax rate, changed little for many taxpayers between 1978 and 1987 because of the 22 percent increase in the payroll tax rate and the 265 percent increase in the payroll tax base (from $16,500 to $43,800).

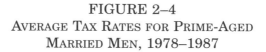

FIGURE 2–4
AVERAGE TAX RATES FOR PRIME-AGED
MARRIED MEN, 1978–1987

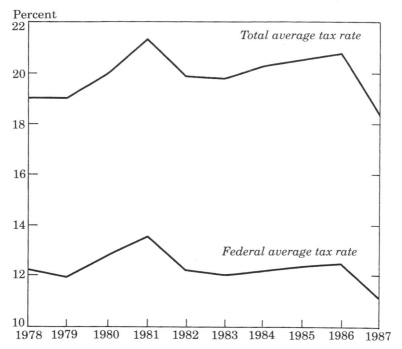

SOURCE: Panel Study of Income Dynamics.

Taken together, figures 2–1 through 2–6 document the substantial changes happening in the U.S. federal tax code during the 1980s so that the potentially stimulative effects of the tax reforms on male labor supply should be readily apparent. Nevertheless, total tax burdens did not fall nearly as much as federal tax burdens, mostly because of the rise of the social security tax that lessened the potentially stimulative effects of the federal reforms.

We now examine what the federal government was predicting would be the effects of the two major reforms

FIGURE 2–5

AVERAGE FEDERAL TAX RATES AFTER TAX REFORM
FOR PRIME-AGED MARRIED MEN, BY INCOME DECILE,
1978, 1982, AND 1987

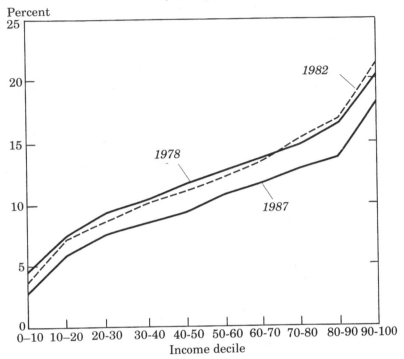

SOURCE: Panel Study of Income Dynamics.

we study, ERTA and TRA86. We use the discussions in the *Economic Report of the President* (1982, 1987) as a record of the official expectations of the effects of the two tax reforms. Comparing our findings with what the President's Council of Economic Advisers (CEA) anticipated indicates the realism of policymakers' ex ante judgments of recent tax reform outcomes and suggests whether our more elaborate empirical approach could produce improved insights into how tax reform influences labor supply and economic well-being.

FIGURE 2–6
AVERAGE TOTAL TAX RATES AFTER TAX REFORM

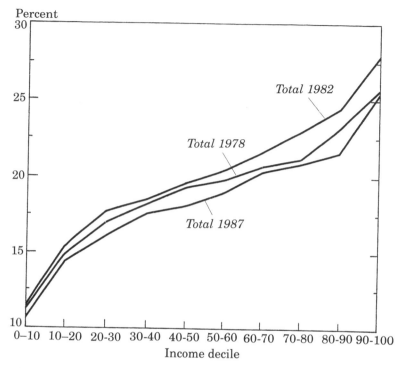

SOURCE: Panel Study of Income Dynamics.

CEA Predictions

In 1982, the CEA clearly recognized that tax reform affects labor supply through the economic returns to work and asset accumulation, albeit sometimes with a somewhat unconventional view that tax-induced increases in the return to any economic activity will raise work effort. The *1982 Economic Report of the President* noted that

> household choices . . . between work and leisure are influenced by after-tax wage rates and after-tax rates of return on capital. When the

government changes either the level or structure of taxes, it ultimately alters household decisions about . . . work effort. . . . Lowering taxes on capital income raises the after-tax return on that income. The larger after-tax return effectively lowers the cost of enjoying leisure as well as consuming in the future relative to the present. Hence, a reduction in taxes on capital income increases the incentive to work now and can thus stimulate the supply of labor." Although the CEA made no specific quantitative predictions of the likely effects of ERTA, it wrote that "the net effect of the tax cut on saving and labor supply will vary according to household circumstances. The preponderance of empirical studies suggests that the labor supply effects of a tax cut are small for married men. (pp. 117–18, 121)

The CEA was willing to issue slightly more specific predictions concerning the economic effects of TRA86 in the *1987 Economic Report of the President*:

The Tax Reform Act of 1986 . . . broadens the personal and corporate income tax bases and substantially lowers tax rates. . . . Lower marginal tax rates on personal income, in conjunction with a broader tax base, will increase labor effort . . . . Estimates that have been made, however, suggest that the Nation's output of goods and services will permanently increase by approximately 2 percent because of the long-run consequences of tax reform. . . . The marginal tax rate on labor income, for example, drives a wedge between the value of output that an additional unit of labor produces and the after-tax wage received by workers, thereby discouraging additional labor effort. A reform of the tax system that lowers the marginal tax rate on labor income, while raising the same total revenue, therefore increases economic well-being. Economic well-being is increased because the value of total output is increased by more than the total value of leisure is decreased. . . . TRA will cut personal income taxes by about 6.6 percent in 1988. . . . The immediate effect of TRA will be to raise the net wage by 6.2 percent and lower the net return to saving by 5.9 percent. These changes will increase labor effort. . . . The point estimates of TRA's long-run effects are . . . [and] labor input rises 3.1 percent. Because the value of consumption is raised more than the value of leisure is decreased, economic welfare is increased. In fact, TRA is estimated to increase individual well-being by as much as would an annual distribution, from an outside source, equal to 1.2 percent of net national product. (pp. 79, 82, 90–92, 93)

Recap. We have summarized the discussion in the *Economic Report of the President* surrounding the major tax reforms of the 1980s, ERTA and TRA86, to establish a benchmark against which our estimates may be compared. We must keep in mind how much our estimates, which come from a more complex empirical framework, differ from estimates produced with the traditional methods applied by the Council of Economic Advisers. Concerning the effects of the two tax reforms of the 1980s, people generally expected the labor supply of married men to increase as much as 6 percent and tax collections to fall by no more than 7 percent. ERTA lowered and flattened tax rates without maintaining an unchanged collection of tax revenue, as was the case of TRA86, so that the effective tax-rate cut under ERTA was double or triple the effective tax-rate cut under TRA86 (*Economic Report of the President* 1982, 1987). We might reasonably expect ERTA to have a welfare effect, then, that is also two to three times that of TRA86, so that together the two tax reforms could be expected to increase economic well-being by up to 5 percent.

We now turn from our discussion to an explanation of how our research framework differs from the approach previously employed by economists in forming the predictions presented in the *Economic Report of the President* concerning ERTA and TRA86.

3

Lifetime Labor Supply
and Taxation

The empirical framework generally underlying previous research on the effects of taxes on labor supply and economic welfare is that of Hausman (1981). He was the first to pay comprehensive statistical attention to the complication that progressive income taxes make the marginal tax rate implicitly a choice of the worker. Hausman's contribution was to find that accounting for the complexity of progressive taxes matters to the estimates of labor supply. Specifically, he found significantly larger effects of wages and capital income on labor supply than previous research did, a finding that enlarges the potential for lower marginal tax rates to increase economic well-being.

More recent research argues that Hausman's approach rests on too many unrealistic assumptions (MaCurdy, Green, and Paarsch 1990). Not only does Hausman's empirical approach require the worker to have knowledge of the entire budget constraint, all tax rates and brackets, but it also requires that the pretax wage and pretax capital market income be independent of the amount of time worked. Most important, Hausman's statistical approach forces his labor supply estimates to be more responsive to tax changes than actually happens in the data. Our empirical approach allows the data more freedom to tell the story than permitted by the statistical model Hausman and followers have applied.

It is also true that much previous research on the work-disincentive effects of income taxation uses conceptualizations in which the worker decides his current labor supply in isolation from things to come. Ignoring the likelihood that workers consider the future when deciding what to do today downplays the distorting effects of progressive income taxes, especially the additional loss of economic well-being from a progressive income tax compared with a tax that collects the same revenue but is not based on a person's income.

The second distinguishing feature of our empirical approach compared with previous research as typified by Hausman's, which underlies the predictions of the effects of tax reform by the Council of Economic Advisers just discussed, is that by incorporating workers' likely consideration of the future consequences of today's actions, we find that income taxes impose a larger economic burden. The interested reader should consult the appendix for more of the theoretical and statistical details of how we infer the effects of the tax reforms, because what follows now is a nontechnical explanation of our approach and findings.

Representations of Lifetime Labor Supply

A major innovation in estimating lifetime labor supply has been to recognize that in an environment of economic certainty, future economic information, such as wealth, can be summarized by a worker-specific constant. The practical implication of being able to collect the influence of unknown future events on labor supply in a single estimable term is that the researcher needs only current economic information to calculate the algebraic equation for labor supply. In the more complicated case of an economic environment where the worker is uncertain about future wages and interest rates, current saving summarizes the worker's future plans, which again simplifies estimating labor supply outcomes. The empirical convenience of estimating labor supply in light of saving behavior is maintained when only wage income is taxed or when there is a flat tax on earnings and capital income. A theoretically valid empirical representation of labor supply becomes more complicated when, as is true in most Western economies, wage and interest incomes are jointly taxed progressively.

Complexities of Joint Taxation

To understand the complications introduced by joint progressive taxation of labor and capital incomes, consider a person who is making consumption and desired work hours choices. If a worker's preferences are linked over the lifetime through habits, and incomes are linked over the lifetime by progressive capital income taxation, then a change in the current wage rate will affect future consumption and labor supply plans through multiple avenues. A change in the wage will (1) alter disposable income and lifetime wealth, which then alters consumption and leisure; (2) alter work incentives and labor supplied, which can in turn alter planned future consumption and labor supply; and (3) alter future after-tax interest rates and wages because of progressive income taxation of future earnings from current investments and saving, which also influences future consumption and labor supply.

If lifetime preferences are not subject to habits, then the influence of a change in wages through changing preference patterns is eliminated, channel (2) above. A proportional tax on income eliminates multiyear connections among wage and capital incomes, (3) above. The lack of multiyear links among both lifetime preferences and disposable incomes makes a change in the current wage rate have only a wealth effect on future labor supply. Most important for our research is that when the worker's preferences and lifetime income are not linked across years, observed saving is sufficient information to infer his future economic plans.

Alternatively, if the researcher wants to examine a realistically progressive tax on wage and capital incomes, then the statistical model must acknowledge that current wage or tax changes will affect the future after-tax wage and return on capital income. Because progressive taxation of all income links disposable incomes across years, a change in the current after-tax wage will affect future labor supplied through both total wealth and the incentive to work. Unlike flat taxes, jointly progressive taxes make the after-tax rate of return on capital income depend on labor supplied now and in the future. Moreover, current labor supply depends on the relationship between future taxes and current saving. A researcher ideally wants to avoid needing the knowledge of all the future wage, tax, and interest rates that may influence lifetime labor supply when there is jointly progressive wage and interest income taxation.

Fortunately, one can estimate the worker's short-run preferences for consumption and income by examining labor supplied in light of assets at the beginning and end of the year. Assets at the beginning of a year capture economically the influence of past decisions, and assets at the end of the year capture economically the influence of next period's expected returns to work and capital accumulation. Data on the household's changing financial position, which will usually be available only in a data base that contains microlongitudinal information, facilitate estimating the lifetime labor supply implications of reforming a relatively inclusive progressive income tax system.

Worker Preferences

We build our empirical examination of worker labor supply and the associated welfare effects of taxes by using a streamlined representation of preferences for work. It is necessary to base the research on a so-called structural model, which means that labor supply has an explicit algebraic connection to an algebraic representation of worker economic well-being, to be able to discuss the welfare implications of tax reform. We (1) assume that a worker's economic well-being is enhanced by an increase in the after-tax real wage and assets; (2) permit workers a desire to avoid risky investments; and (3) allow a role for observable personal demographic characteristics to influence preferences for work versus leisure and current versus future incomes. Our two-step multivariate statistical procedure first estimates short-run labor supply preferences and then uses the estimates to infer the long-run labor supply preferences needed to predict the lifetime responsiveness of labor supply to economic influences. We purposely select the algebraic form describing worker preferences that connects to the popular linear labor supply equation, thus facilitating comparisons of our results with past research on the effects of taxes on labor supply.

4
Estimating Income Tax Effects

C ross-sectional data, which offer information on a set of workers at a common point in time, are sufficient to estimate the coefficients in an algebraic equation describing a person's short-run work preferences. Identifying both short-run and long-run preferences requires either longitudinal data, which provide information on a common set of workers followed over time, or, less ideally, several cross-sections of sufficiently similar workers during several different years. The longitudinal data we use facilitate accounting for both observed and unobserved worker differences in willingness to work.

Progressive Taxes

We noted earlier that the most influential empirical research on the labor supply effects of the U.S. progressive federal tax system has applied a statistical procedure resting on strong behavioral assumptions, including the assumption that a worker has complete knowledge of all tax brackets and that the pretax wage and nonwage income are independent of hours worked. Pretax wages will depend on hours worked because researchers typically use average hourly earnings to measure the rate of pay. If hours worked are measured with error, then average hourly earnings are measured with error too, and average hourly earnings become arithmetically related to hours worked. It has also recently been noted that some of the most influential research has used models that force a non-negative estimated wage effect and a nonpositive estimated income effect on labor supplied. Our empirical procedure adds the realism of progressive capital income taxation along with allowing observed behavior to imply more of the labor supply story than previous research has permitted.

Our statistical approach simplifies matters by requiring information only on the effective marginal tax rate. Reported taxable income is relatively free of measurement error in the typical microdata set. The advantage of beginning with the accurate information on overall taxable income is that the marginal tax rate can then be closely tracked by a single continuous curved line, which can also be used to infer the total taxes needed to calculate the worker's net wealth.

Using a cubic algebraic equation to describe the effective set of federal income taxes in the United States readily accommodates the fact that social security taxes apply only to a portion of earnings. Moreover, during the period we study most states had progressive income tax schedules. About three-fourths of the states used federal adjusted gross income or federal taxable income as their tax bases. We believe that the impact of state income taxes is too important to ignore but too complicated to represent exhaustively. Because we focus on how federal income taxes affect lifetime labor supply, we augment the worker's federal marginal tax and social security tax rates with an average state tax rate defined as the ratio of individual state income tax collections to adjusted gross income in the state.

5

Data

Our data cover 1978–1987 and come from the Panel Study of Income Dynamics, the data source used in the most influential empirical research on labor supply in the United States. We selected our sample using multiple criteria similar to ones used by others studying the labor supply of prime-aged males. The workers in our study are men who were continuously married and worked each year during 1978–1987. The men were ages twenty-two to fifty-one in 1978, so that they were out of school but not yet retired, which allows us to avoid the statistical complexities introduced by schooling and retirement. The worker must have been paid either an hourly wage rate or a salary; we deleted piece-rate and self-employed workers to sidestep the problem of inferring an hourly wage for men whose pay is not formally tied to time at work. Our sample selection process yielded 532 prime-aged U.S. men with the relevant information over the ten years we study. Table 5–1 summarizes the information we use to estimate taxation's effect on labor supply and economic well-being.

Wages

The Panel Study of Income Dynamics asks workers how they are paid. For workers paid by the hour, the

TABLE 5–1
SUMMARY STATISTICS FOR CONTINUOUSLY WORKING MEN
AGES 22 TO 51 IN 1978, 1978–1987

Variable	Mean	Standard Deviation
Annual hours of work	2182.55	492.06
Reported gross wage	14.89	7.29
Reported net wage	10.22	4.14
Average gross hourly earnings	15.64	8.76
Average net hourly earnings	10.75	5.83
Marginal tax rate (%)	29.00	7.00
Liquid assets[a]	15084.28	50790.11
Home equity	49196.25	54109.15
Total wealth	64280.53	81276.85
Virtual wealth	78879.81	90181.21
Net saving	3867.78	62743.19
Virtual saving	5188.94	62893.29
Gross 3-month T-bill rate (%)	3.00	2.00
Net 3-month T-bill rate (%)	0.30	2.00
Age	38.92	8.45
Children	1.56	1.20
Grades completed	13.19	2.60
Race (1 = white)	0.92	0.27
Homeowner (1 = yes)	0.89	0.32

NOTE: Number of observations in sample = 5,320. All wealth, price, and income variables are in real terms with respect to the 1987 personal consumption expenditure deflator.

a. Liquid assets equal nominal interest, dividend, and rental income earnings with the first $200 deflated by the average annual passbook saving rate and the remainder deflated by the average annual 3-month T-bill rate.

SOURCE: Panel Study of Income Dynamics.

survey records the gross hourly wage rate. The inter-
viewer asks salaried workers how frequently they are
paid, such as weekly, biweekly, or monthly. The survey
then norms a salaried worker's pay by a fixed number
of hours depending on the pay period. Salary divided
by forty, for example, is the hourly wage rate constructed for a salaried worker who is paid weekly. The
estimated labor supply response in previous research
using average hourly earnings as the relevant rate of
pay suffers from what has been termed negative division bias, because the explanatory variable of interest
(average hourly earnings) contains in its denominator
the outcome being studied (hours worked). The pretax
hourly wage rate we use is maximally free of division
bias.

Taxes

When constructing annual taxable income, we presume
that the married men we study filed joint tax returns.
Adjusted gross income is the sum of the man's labor
earnings plus capital market income. Taxable income is
adjusted gross income less deductions and exemptions.
The Panel Study of Income Dynamics provides the number of tax exemptions for dependents taken in each
year, but how we calculate deductions merits additional
discussion.

1978–1983. Computing the value of deductions depends
on the year being considered. To evaluate deductions for
years up to and including 1983, we followed the conven-
tion of the Panel Study of Income Dynamics. With
yearly information from the Internal Revenue Service's
Statistics of Income, we generated the typical value of
itemized deductions based on the man's adjusted gross
income. We then calculated the difference between typical itemized deductions and the standard deduction,

known as excess itemized deductions. For the years up to and including 1983, when excess itemized deductions were positive, we subtracted excess itemized deductions from adjusted gross income; when excess itemized deductions were not positive, we applied the standard deduction.

1984–1987. Beginning in 1984, the PSID records whether the family itemized deductions. For known itemizers, we subtracted excess itemized deductions from adjusted gross income and used the standard deduction for the men who did not itemize deductions. Before the Tax Reform Act of 1986, the standard deduction was built into the tax tables, so that we only need subtract from taxable income the value of deductions exceeding the standard deduction. Since TRA86, the standard deduction is no longer built into the tax tables, so we subtracted either the standard deduction or the total itemized deductions from adjusted gross income depending on whether the family itemized.

As noted previously, the worker's effective marginal tax rate is his state income tax rate plus the federal marginal tax rate and the social security tax rate when applicable. We used a cubic equation to summarize the set of federal income tax rates. To elaborate using 1978 as an example, there are fifteen marginal tax brackets between taxable incomes of $3,200 and $67,200. Taking $50 increments in incomes $3,200 to $67,200 and calculating the associated statutory marginal tax rates in 1978 yields 1,280 pairs of incomes and marginal tax rates. A cubic equation connecting the 1,280 marginal tax rate–income pairs summarizes the 1978 federal tax table for married couples filing jointly. The curvilinear cubic equation we use to describe the U.S. progressive federal income tax structure for 1978 accounts for 98 percent of the variation in tax rates across $50 increments in income and is depicted in figure 5–1.

FIGURE 5–1
STATUTORY AND SMOOTH MARGINAL TAX RATES, FOR
PRIME-AGED MARRIED MEN, WITH INCOMES OF
$0 TO $78,850

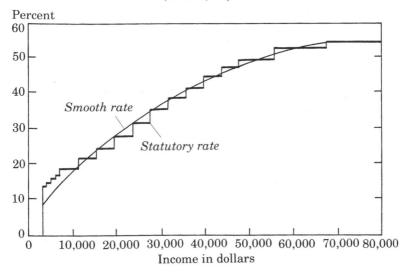

SOURCE: Panel Study of Income Dynamics.

The first year of our sample, 1978, provides an example of how we build the marginal tax rate for a married couple filing jointly. First, we take note of the zero bracket amount in the tax schedule. For taxable income above zero but less than $3,200, the marginal tax rate is the state tax rate plus the payroll tax rate of 6.05 percent. When taxable income hits $3,200, the worker faces the federal marginal tax rate in the cubic equation depicted in figure 5–1 plus the other effective taxes. When taxable income hits $67,200, the effective marginal tax rate is the sum of the 1978 maximum federal rate of 55 percent, the state income tax rate, and the payroll tax rate if gross labor earnings were below $17,000.

Assets

As is the case with most data sets, the Panel Study of Income Dynamics has little information on interest rates, assets, and saving. When an interest rate is needed to estimate how the worker behaves as his net wealth accumulates, we use the after-tax annual average three-month Treasury bill interest rate. We constructed assets as the sum of the liquid and illiquid asset measures in the PSID. Liquid assets are nominal rent, interest, and dividend income divided by a nominal interest rate to create a capital value or implicit principal underlying the annual asset income received. We created a capital value for the first $200 of income from liquid assets using the annual average passbook savings account rate and created a capital value for rental income in excess of $200 per year using the annual average interest rate on three-month Treasury bills. For the illiquid component of assets, we used the value of home equity defined as the difference between house value and outstanding principal remaining. Unlike previous researchers, we included illiquid assets because in our sample almost 90 percent of the men are homeowners, but only about half the men have any liquid wealth.

The measure of total wealth from the PSID has been used by others. Our summary wealth statistics are comparable to wealth measures from other extensive surveys of income and assets, such as the Survey of Income and Program Participation. Moreover, the PSID collected comprehensive wealth data in 1984 and 1989, including data on house equity, net value of other real estate, net value of vehicles, net value of a farm or other business, and net value of other assets. Variation in our measure of liquid wealth explains about half the variation in total wealth, and including home equity makes the variation in our measure of wealth explain about 80 percent of the variation in total wealth. The ability of our wealth measure to track total wealth when measured independently is the justification for including both liquid and illiquid components in our measure of wealth.

6

How Wages and Taxes
Affect Labor Supply

Our empirical research first estimates short-run labor supply responses to the after-tax wage and asset income to identify short-run preferences for work. Next we estimate the quantitative properties of long-run preferences building on the quantitative properties of short-run preferences estimated first. In both stages, we allow for possible interpersonal differences in work effort that are not reflected in observable personal characteristics. Finally, we use the estimates of prime-aged men's short-run and long-run preferences for work to compute their lifetime preferences and resulting sensitivity of labor supply to changes in wages, assets, and taxes.

Short-Run Responses

Our multivariate model allows the need for a worker to anticipate certain current economic events and for the influence of demographics in deciding labor supplied, such as age, health, and number of children living at home. In taking account of the economic uncertainty that influences labor market decisions, we assume that the worker uses expectations formed with information that includes his age, education, number of children, health, union membership, home ownership, rate of pay, income taxes, interest rates, and after-tax wealth. We chose the set of information that workers are assumed to use to describe their economic environment in part to maintain similarity with previous empirical research on labor supply. The information set we assume that workers use to anticipate uncertain current economic events has statistically acceptable predictive power.

The most statistically trustworthy estimate of how labor supply responds to wages and taxes comes from our empirical framework. In that framework, the information that workers take into account in making decisions includes possible macroeconomic disturbances, the pretax wage is influenced by work effort through avenues such as premium pay for overtime, and the wage is most accurately measured as the hourly rate of pay workers themselves report. We find that hours of work decline with marginal tax rates but not as a simple mirror image of wage changes because of the future consequences of how work effort affects current capital accumulation and in turn the future tax rate.

We estimate that, on average, a prime-aged married man would work about 1 to 2 percent more in the short run in response to a 10 percent increase in his after-tax wage. The estimated effect of a change in the income from financial assets is tiny; a 10 percent larger after-tax capital market income would lower labor supplied by only about 0.2 percent. Hours worked by a prime-aged married man would fall slightly more than 0.5 percent in the short run with each 10 percent increase in U.S. marginal tax rates.

Long-Run Responses

The second step of our research builds on our estimates of how workers respond to wage and tax changes in the short run. Treating the estimated short-run labor supply equation as known for the purposes of estimation, we proceed to infer labor supply and long-run preferences for income and work, including how a prime-aged married man subjectively discounts future economic events and how much he dislikes economic risk, which are key underpinnings of lifetime labor supply outcomes. We attempt to enrich the research design over what has been done previously by allowing for interpersonal differences in the worker's subjective discount rate and for the worker's formation of expectations of the economic future in a way that accounts not only for his wage and tax rate currently in effect but also for the temporal patterns of interest rates, health, home ownership, and total wealth. The set of information we assume workers use to anticipate their economic future has statistically acceptable predictive power. Finally, we note that our representation of labor supply decisions assumes that the worker has so-called rational expectations of uncertain economic outcomes, which implies that past mistakes in predicting economic outcomes, such as the interest rate, do not influence long-run decisions. Our statistical results are consistent with the typical prime-aged man having rational, or correct on average, expectations of his long-run economic future.

As an aside, we note our findings that the average value we estimate for the person-specific discount rates indicates that our typical man uses an implicit interest rate of 1 to 2 percent to devalue the future. The average implicit interest rate we estimate that men use to compare their economic future with the present is in the middle of the range of estimates in the empirical literature on consumption. The average man in our study is averse to economic risk, and his aversion to fluctuating income increases with lifetime wealth accumulation.

Because of its relevance to economic policy, a focal point of the empirical literature on lifetime labor supply has been the labor supply response to an anticipated permanent wage change. Because its effect on lifetime wealth is relatively small, a permanent lifetime wage increase has a labor supply effect similar to the effect of an increase in the current year's wage alone. A 10 percent increase in lifetime wages increases annual lifetime labor supplied by about 1 to 2 percent in our data.

The responsiveness of lifetime labor supplied to wages varies significantly across economic strata. We find that the labor supply response to a tax-induced wage change rises with wealth. The response of lifetime hours to wage changes is about 40 percent larger for the wealthiest 25 percent compared with the poorest 25 percent of prime-aged married men. As wealth increases, so does a worker's responsiveness to taxation. The percentage response to changes in the marginal tax rate doubles as one moves from the lowest to the highest wealth quartile. A greater labor supply responsiveness to wage changes for wealthier families happens for two reasons. First, higher-wage workers are more responsive to wage changes, and wages are on average 40 percent higher in the highest wealth quartile than in the lowest wealth quartile. Second, labor supplied is more responsive to the tax rate at higher wealth levels such that the marginal tax-rate effect is not the same across workers. The labor supply response to taxes differs by 100 percent between the lowest and the highest wealth quartiles.

We now examine in more depth how wealth interacts with tax reforms. Our results emphasize that studying only the average labor supply response obscures some interesting distributional consequences of tax policy.

7

Evaluating the Reforms
of the 1980s

We now use our estimates of worker preferences as revealed by their labor supply outcomes to calculate so-called exact measures of the changes in economic well-being due to changes in the U.S. income tax laws during the 1980s. Our objective is to understand how the additional reality of statistically acknowledging jointly progressive taxation of labor and capital incomes sharpens the estimated labor supply and welfare-enhancing effects of tax policies that generally lower and flatten income tax rates. In particular, we quantify the economic benefits of the tax reforms of the 1980s in the United States by calculating a payment that the typical prime-aged married working man could make to the government that would leave his economic welfare unchanged after he adjusts his work behavior to the new tax structure.

Inferring the Economic Effects

In calculating the implied changes in economic well-being, we first predict the labor supply responses to four federal income tax reforms. Because labor supply depends on the progressive income tax schedule, the applicable marginal tax rate is codetermined with hours worked. To be consistent with past research, our predictions take spouses' labor supply decisions as sequential in the sense that the husband chooses his labor supply without regard to his wife's work preferences. In the sequential decision-making process, the wife's labor and interest incomes do not contribute to the husband's marginal tax-rate calculations used in his work plans. The wife then chooses her labor supply, and her actual earnings codetermine the family's applicable tax rate through the household's joint taxable income and future capital earnings from saving. In our calculations of how taxes affect lifetime labor supply, most of the predicted labor supply adjustments happen in the first year. We use our estimates of workers' short-run preferences for work to predict labor supplied, wealth accumulation, the marginal tax rate, and tax payments, which we then use to infer how four tax reforms enhance economic well-being.

Four Tax Regime Changes

Table 7–1 presents our calculations of the relative welfare effects of four U.S. federal tax regimes: (1) the 1987 (post-TRA86) U.S. income tax structure compared with an economy where taxes are absent; (2) the 1987 U.S. income tax structure compared with a 10 percent across-the-board rate cut; (3) the 1987 income tax rates compared with the 1981 (pre-ERTA) income tax regime; and (4) the 1987 income tax rates and tax base compared with the pre-ERTA income tax regime. Because our conceptual and natural experiments are tax cuts, all welfare implications are calculations of the maximum amounts that a prime-aged married working man would pay the federal government to lower his tax rates. The particular tax reform and the worker's location in the wealth distribution determine labor supply,

TABLE 7–1
HOURS AND WELFARE EFFECTS OF ALTERNATIVE TAX REFORMS, BY WEALTH QUARTILE

	Change in Hours	Change in Tax Payments (percent)	Equivalent Variation[a]	Welfare Variation[a]
		No-Tax Case		
Average	4.01	–100.00	–22.48	–22.83
1st quartile	2.49	–100.00	–17.18	–17.33
2nd quartile	2.82	–100.00	–17.46	–17.59
3rd quartile	3.94	–100.00	–20.50	–20.72
4th quartile	6.94	–100.00	–30.14	–30.80
		10 Percent Tax Cut		
Average	0.61	–6.28	–2.09	–2.11
1st quartile	0.02	–9.25	–1.67	–1.68
2nd quartile	0.68	–8.73	–1.65	–1.66
3rd quartile	0.62	–7.41	–1.89	–1.91
4th quartile	1.13	–4.53	–2.73	–2.79

Pre-ERTA to Post-TRA86 Tax Rate Cut

Average	2.05	−37.56	−11.02	−11.24
1st quartile	1.71	−40.57	−8.64	−8.75
2nd quartile	1.01	−39.69	−9.06	−9.16
3rd quartile	2.04	−39.32	−10.37	−10.53
4th quartile	3.54	−35.49	−14.11	−14.51

Pre-ERTA to Post-TRA86 Tax Rate and Base Cut

Average	3.12	−46.17	−15.64	−15.93
1st quartile	2.39	−49.53	−13.79	−13.96
2nd quartile	2.30	−45.87	−13.80	−13.96
3rd quartile	2.93	−44.43	−15.28	−15.51
4th quartile	4.98	−45.96	−18.14	−18.63

a. Percentage of his adjusted gross income that the average prime-aged married working man would pay to have the tax reform under consideration.

SOURCE: Panel Study of Income Dynamics.

with the greatest response coming from the wealthiest workers.

Eliminating Income Taxes. We begin with the popular benchmark of the total labor supply effects and gain in economic well-being from eliminating income taxes. Eliminating the income taxes that existed in 1987 would have led prime-aged married men to work about 4 percent more on average, an estimate that is 60 percent larger than the estimate from a labor supply model where workers are assumed to make decisions for only one year at a time. Workers in the upper quartile of the wealth distribution would have supplied about 7 percent more labor. The typical prime-aged married male worker in the United States would pay 20–25 percent of his adjusted gross income to eliminate the progressive income taxation that existed in 1987.

As an additional reference point, we note that Hausman's widely cited estimates of the labor supply effects of removing income taxes are about 8 percent higher than ours, and his estimates of a man's willingness to pay for replacing income-based taxation with an equivalent income-neutral tax are 2 percent lower than ours. Hausman's estimates are driven by a large income effect that discourages work effort, and our calculations have a larger estimated lifetime work incentive effect. By adding progressive capital income taxation to a lifetime decision process with two additional bits of realism—(1) worker heterogeneity that is unrelated to observed demographic characteristics and (2) an income stream that is interconnected across years by income taxes that apply to capital income—we locate a greater extent of the economic burden of income taxes than Hausman.

A 10 Percent Across-the-Board Rate Cut. A second popular benchmark in discussing tax reform is to calculate the implications of a substantial, but not over-whelming, cut in all marginal tax rates, such as 10 per-cent. A 10 percent across-the-board rate cut from the 1987 tax structure would lead to about a 0.6 percent increase in the labor supplied annually by prime-aged married men (about thirteen hours) accompanied by a reduction in government tax revenues of about 6 per-cent. Our typical working married man would pay 1 to 2 percent of his adjusted gross income to have a 10 per-cent cut in the tax rate. The wealthiest 25 percent of men would each pay 2 to 3 percent of their AGI for a 10 percent reduction in income tax rates.

The small response in the typical man's labor sup-ply to a 10 percent tax cut indicates that the stimulative effects of the recent Dole-Kemp 15 percent across-the-board tax cut proposed during the 1996 presidential race would likely be much smaller than suggested by the candidates.

ERTA and the TRA86 Tax-Rate Cut. Our penulti-mate calculations compare the labor supply response and change in economic burden associated with mov-ing from the pre-ERTA (1981) income tax regime to the post-TRA86 (1987) income tax rates. The average prime-aged married male worker raised hours sup-plied by 2 percent and would have paid 11 percent of his adjusted gross income for the change to TRA86's tax rates. To emphasize the distributional implications of the differing elasticities, we note our result that the wealthiest workers increased their labor supplied by about 4 percent and had about a 14 percent improve-ment in their economic well-being due to ERTA and the tax rates under TRA86 compared with the pre-ERTA tax regime. The labor supply response of the wealthiest workers is about 100 percent, and the wel-fare effect about 33 percent greater than the average worker's.

ERTA and the TRA86 Tax Rate and Base Cuts. Our final calculation compares how labor supply and the economic burden of the U.S progressive income tax changed by moving from the pre-ERTA (1981) income tax regime to the post-TRA86 (1987) income tax rates and base. TRA86 took over 6 million people off the tax rolls so that including both the tax rate and the base changes makes the predicted hours-worked response higher than when ignoring the tax base changes under TRA86. Again, it is important to note the distributional implications of our results, which are the more substantial labor supply response and welfare effects for the wealthiest workers compared with the poorest or average workers.

The dual effects of the rate and base changes under TRA86 are a 2–5 percent increase in labor supplied across the four wealth quartiles. As a benchmark, actual hours worked increased by 3–4 percent during 1981–1987. Comparing our predicted outcomes with and without the changes in the tax base under the 1986 tax reforms suggests the tax base effect of TRA86. Changes in the tax base under TRA86 increased both average labor supplied and the welfare improvement under TRA86 by about an additional 50 percent with the largest effects, again, in the two lowest wealth quartiles.

Our estimates of the reduction in tax payments are roughly 40 percent larger than the Council of Economic Advisers' projection of a 25 percent reduction in tax payments. One source of difference is that our calculations are based on the pre-ERTA 1981 tax rates, a period when the so-called bracket creep pushed average marginal tax rates up to their highest level in our sample period, whereas the CEA apparently based its calculations on the lower post-ERTA tax rates. Another source of difference between our calculations and the CEA's discussed in chapter 2 is that our calculations are based solely on continuously working married men. To the extent that ERTA and TRA86 induced new entrants into the labor force, tax payments will not fall to the extent that our empirical model predicts.

8
Implications for Future Research

Our research develops a realistic, but still manageable, representation of lifetime labor supply outcomes by workers who pay a progressive income tax covering both earnings from work and capital income, which creates multiyear links in disposable incomes. Using data for prime-aged married working men during 1978–1987 from the Panel Study of Income Dynamics and a curvilinear representation of the set of federal income taxes, our empirical procedure first infers short-run and then long-run worker preferences for income and work. We use our labor supply estimates to calculate the welfare gains due to tax reforms during the 1980s that produced a flatter federal income tax structure in the United States. We find that although ERTA and TRA86 lowered total tax payments, they stimulated the labor supplied by prime-aged men by about 3 percent and reduced the economic burden of progressive income taxation by about 16 percent.

If we assume for convenience that coefficients are unchanging over time, our model can also be used to simulate or project the responses of labor supply to other tax reforms. In 1993 President Clinton proposed and Congress passed legislation that increased the marginal tax rates of the highest-income Americans by almost a third. The crucial argument offered by proponents of the tax increase was that labor supply would be left relatively unchanged. To examine whether the president and Congress were correct in claiming that the highest-income workers respond little to the changed work incentives, we increased the top marginal tax rate in the last year of our sample, 1987, also by about a third, from 38.5 percent to 50.1 percent. We then computed the labor supply and tax payments for the upper two percentiles of the gross income distribution. Our framework projects that labor supply would fall by about 2 percent and tax payments would fall by as much as 9 percent for the uppermost segment of the income distribution. The lesson to be gained is that labor supply and tax revenues are most responsive to changes in the tax code for the highest-income earners, so that the argument that tax collections will rise proportionately with tax rates is least realistic for the top taxpayers.

A proposal that has received on-again-off-again attention among policy makers and such presidential hopefuls as Jerry Brown in 1992 and Steve Forbes in 1996 is the flat tax. Numerous variants of the flat tax have been proposed, and the one we consider briefly now is by Robert E. Hall and Alvin Rabushka (1995). The key elements of the Hall-Rabushka plan are to replace the current rate schedule with two marginal tax rates, 0 and 19 percent, and to replace itemized deductions with an expanded standard deduction ($16,500 in 1995) and personal exemption ($4,500 per dependent in 1995). We use our conceptual framework to simulate the labor supply adjustment by replacing the 1987 tax system with the Hall-Rabushka system (expressing the standard deduction and personal exemption in 1987 dollars) and calculating the resulting labor supply and tax revenue changes. According to our results, the flat tax would increase the labor supplied by upper-income

Americans by about 2 percent in the fourth quartile of the wealth distribution and by about 10 percent in the ninety-eighth percentile of the income distribution. We find that under the Hall-Rabushka flat tax proposal, tax collections from the high wealth or income groups would fall dramatically, by about a third in the fourth wealth quartile and about two-thirds in the ninety-eighth income percentile. In total, our model predicts that if the United States were to adopt the Hall-Rabushka proposed flat tax as its federal income tax, the labor supply of the typical prime-aged married male worker would remain basically unchanged (increase 0.4 percent), while average tax payments would fall by about 23 percent.

Our finding that the flat tax is neutral overall with respect to labor supply conflicts with the predictions offered by the proponents of the flat tax. What is the source of the neutrality of labor supply to the flat tax of Hall and Rabushka? Again, distributional issues are important. The flat tax lowers the marginal tax rate both for low-income earners, who do not respond much to tax reforms, and for high-income earners, who respond positively to tax reforms. Key, though, is that the flat tax raises marginal tax rates for a substantial segment of the population, persons in the second and third wealth quartiles, reducing their labor input. With a skewed distribution of income, more taxpayers are located in the parts of the wealth distribution with either no behavioral response or a negative labor supply response because their tax rates are raised, which makes the general effect of the Hall-Rabushka flat tax proposal neutral toward the overall labor supply.

For readers interested in the comparative implications of our more elaborate conceptual framework, our estimated effect of capital market income on annual labor supply is more modest than the income effects a researcher would produce with the Hausman model.

Moreover, economists calculate the effect of a wage change on labor supply that is net of any effect on the worker's total income by subtracting the estimated capital income effect on labor supply from the estimated overall wage effect on labor supply. The larger estimated income effect produced with the Hausman approach accompanies a larger estimated net (of income effect) wage effect on annual labor supply than we find. Economists calculate the worker's willingness to pay for a tax reform at a given level of real income. The larger estimated income-compensated wage effect calculated with the Hausman approach then also makes the estimated short-run effects of income taxation on economic well-being larger than ours. Although our estimate of the effect of progressive income taxation on economic well-being is lower than previous researchers' for a single year, our estimate of the total welfare-enhancing effect of tax reform is greater because we use a lifetime perspective. The popular Hausman method implicitly underlying the CEA estimates, which does not fully account for lifetime decisions, indicates a welfare increase from the tax reforms of the 1980s that is about a third the size of our calculation presented at the bottom of table 7–1.

Moreover, our statistical results reject an empirical representation of labor supply that assumes away the multi-year connections in disposable incomes by ignoring capital income taxation. Our research suggests that future studies of the work-incentive effects of income taxes would benefit from using longitudinal data, which permit including the empirical realism of worker differences in the willingness to work that are not related to observable personal characteristics, and from acknowledging that labor market decisions are made subject to joint progressive taxation of wage and capital income.

The literature still lacks models of lifetime behavior that permit tax-induced effects on the labor-force-participation decision in conjunction with the hours-of-work decision, which is particularly important to the study of the behavior of women's labor supply. Similarly missing is research on taxation and models of household members' joint behaviors. Conceptualizations of dual decisions by spouses face formidable technical challenges in light of the critiques by Apps and Rees (1997) and Chiappori (1997), who argue against the practical realism of assuming that spouses pool their resources and behave according to a single set of objectives. There is still much work to be done because research on the labor market effects of taxation is still closer to a toddler than a senior citizen on the maturity spectrum.

Technical Appendix

The appendix that follows summarizes the technical details of our two-step empirical conceptual framework describing lifetime labor supply with a progressive income tax on all income.

Short-Run Work Preferences

Our two-step empirical approach begins with a linear labor supply equation for the typical worker that is

$$h_t = \alpha\omega_t + \delta A_{t-1} + \phi A_t + X_t\gamma + \eta + \xi_t, \qquad \text{(A–1)}$$

where h_t is hours worked. The amount of labor supplied depends on the real after-tax marginal wage rate, $\omega_t = W_t(1 - \tau(I_t))$, the equation for the marginal tax rate, $\tau(I_t)$, which depends on taxable income, I_t, recent and current assets, A_{t-1} and A_t, a set of fixed and time-varying demographic characteristics influencing short-run preferences for work, which we symbolize as X_t, and a purely random disturbance to hours worked, ξ_t. The Greek letters α, δ, ϕ, γ, and η are coefficients or constants revealed by the data that describe how changes in the associated independent variable influence the person's hours of work for pay. Current and lagged assets reflect extra-period economic influences because they connect earnings to future taxes through saving and the resulting future capital income.

The Marginal Tax Rate. In algebraically describing the labor supply response to changes in the after-tax wage, we use the approach of MaCurdy, Green, and Paarsch (1990) and write the overall marginal tax rate as a curvilinear equation with the person's taxable income, I_t, as its argument

$$\tau_t = [\Phi_{1t} - \Phi_{2t}]\tau_{st} + [\Phi_{2t} - \Phi_{3t}]b(I_t)$$
$$+ \Phi_{3t}\tau_T + \Phi_{sst}\tau_{sst}. \qquad (A-2)$$

The average state income tax rate is τ_{st}, and $b(I_t)$ is a polynomial equation that we will formulate with taxable income as its argument. The largest possible total income tax rate is $\tau_T = \tau_{st} + \tau_{ut}$ where τ_{ut} is the symbol for the uppermost federal marginal tax rate in year t, and τ_{sst} is the symbol for the social security payroll tax rate. In the marginal tax-rate equation, (A-2), $\Phi_{jt}[(I_t - \mu_{jt})/\sigma_{jt}]$ $(j = 1,2,3)$ is the algebraic equation for the cumulative distribution function (CDF) of the standard normal probability distribution. Specifically, $\Phi_{jt}[\bullet]$ is an indicator equation that equals 1 when $I_t \geq \mu_{jt}$ and equals 0 when $I_t < \mu_{jt}$. What the equation $\Phi_{jt}[\bullet]$ does in practice is to keep track of the worker's applicable tax bracket because μ_j is the income level where the tax bracket begins. The speed at which a worker switches from one marginal tax bracket to another marginal tax bracket is determined by σ, with greater speed (smoothness) produced by larger values of σ. In practice, a value of 0.2 for σ in (A-2) worked well. The parallel indicator equation for social security taxes is $\Phi_{sst}[(\mu_{sst} - Y_t)/\sigma_{sst}]$, where μ_{sst} is the dollar cutoff for the social security tax base, and Y_t is labor earnings. A worker's marginal tax rate is then the state income tax rate, τ_{st}, plus the federal marginal tax rate and the social security tax rate.

Instrumental Variables Estimation. When estimating labor supply, we acknowledge that the after-tax wage and assets implicitly depend on labor supplied, because the marginal tax rate depends on contemporaneous hours worked through their links to taxable and after-tax earnings. Any latent worker-specific differences in the willingness to supply labor, η, will generally not be independent of the factors that explain labor supply, which are the wage, assets, and worker demographic characteristics, because lifetime wealth depends on the willingness to work. A convenient statistical approach is to treat latent worker willingness to work as a constant that differs uniquely across persons and to remove it by examining the change in labor supply from year to year. That is, a straightforward way to estimate the coefficients of interest to tax policy research, which are α, δ, ϕ, and γ, is to estimate how $h_t - h_{t-1}$ depends on the changes in the independent variables, $\omega_t - \omega_{t-1}$, $A_t - A_{t-1}$, $A_{t-1} - A_{t-2}$, and $X_t - X_{t-1}$. Because the changes in the stochastic disturbance affecting the change in labor supply, $\xi_t - \xi_{t-1}$, may not be purely random, we correct the standard errors of our first step's estimated coefficients for a changing disturbance that may be correlated over time or vary differently across workers.

Examining labor supply with the change in hours worked, $h_t - h_{t-1}$, as the outcome affects our choice of instruments for, or variables that explain, the codetermined changes in the wage and assets, $\omega_t - \omega_{t-1}$ and $A_t - A_{t-1}$. That is, noneconomic variables (age and health) from a year ago or more and economic variables (wages and assets) from two or more years ago are valid instruments. In our statistically dominant specification, the set of instruments includes (1) indicator variables for each different year; (2) information for each of the two previous years on age, age^2, (age*education), number of children, whether disabled, union membership, and home ownership; and (3) information from two years ago on the gross real wage, the net real wage, the net three-month Treasury bill interest rate, net real wealth, and net virtual wealth, which is actual wealth adjusted upward for the fact that under a progressive income tax, total taxes paid are less than the marginal tax rate times taxable income.

Long-Run Work Preferences

In the second step of our empirical procedure, we estimate the typical prime-aged married male worker's long-run preferences concerning work and income. We rely on the equation describing how the perspicacious person prefers to equalize the year-to-year changes in his economic well-being from wealth (dis)accumulation to understand the underlying lifetime economic choices. Someone with so-called rational expectations will try to maintain

$$[\beta(1 + r_{n,t+1})\lambda_{At+1}] = \lambda_{At}\varepsilon_{t+1}, \qquad (A–3)$$

where $\beta \equiv (1 + \rho)^{-1}$ is the subjective discount factor, $r_{n,t+1} \equiv (1 - \tau_{t+1})r_{t+1}$ is the after-tax (net) real interest rate, λ_{At} is the change in economic well-being from a change in net wealth, and the stochastic disturbance, ε_{t+1}, is any random mistake the worker makes in forecasting how his well-being will change. To apply (A–3), we develop an algebraic expression for the change in economic well-being due to a change in net wealth using a specific equation for worker well-being, also known as utility, that has unknown coefficients describing long-run preferences.

The links among the utility-enhancing effects of changes in the wage and assets and labor supply, known as Roy's Identity, let one pin down the algebraic expression for short-run well-being as $V_t = e^{\delta\omega_t}[A_t + (\alpha/\phi)\omega_t + (X_t\gamma)/\phi + (\delta/\phi)A_{t-1} - (\alpha/\phi^2)]$. The algebraic equation describing short-run economic welfare just developed is how we evaluate the effect of the recent U.S. tax reforms on worker economic well-being. We use our first-step estimate of short-run economic welfare as though all the coefficients were known with certainty and take what is called a Box-Cox algebraic transformation, $B_t(\bullet)$, of short-run preferences, which gives

$$B_t(\underline{V_t}) = \{[V_t(\omega_t, A_t, A_{t-1}; \underline{\underline{\Delta}})]^{(1 + \sigma_t)} - 1\}/(1 + \sigma_t). \quad (A\text{--}4)$$

$V_t(\bullet)$ is an algebraic equation that is increasing in the net real wage and assets that also depends on the estimated coefficient (denoted by a double underline, $\underline{\underline{}}$) describing short-run preferences $\underline{\underline{\Delta}} = [\underline{\underline{\alpha}}, \underline{\underline{\delta}}, \phi, \gamma]$. The $\sigma_t s$ in (A–4) are the unknown coefficients describing long-run preferences, which determine saving and the lifetime pattern of wealth accumulation. We permit long-run preferences to depend on a total of k different observable time-varying demographic variables, Z_{kt}, by using $\sigma_t = \sigma_0 + \Sigma_k \sigma_k Z_{kt}$, which allows the aversion to economic risk to differ across workers.

Taking logarithms (denoted by ln), which facilitates looking at proportionate year-to-year changes in economic well-being, and then using the rule guiding optimal saving (A–3) and the expression for lifetime preferences (A–4), we reach the equation we use to estimate long-run preferences

$$\sigma_0 \Delta ln \underline{V}_{t+1} + \Sigma_k \sigma_k \Delta(Z_{k,t+1} ln \underline{V}_{t+1})$$
$$+ \Delta ln(\underline{\underline{d}}\underline{V}_{t+1}) + \kappa_{t+1} = ln \varepsilon_{t+1}. \quad (A\text{--}5)$$

$\Delta ln \underline{V}_{t+1} = ln \underline{V}_{t+1} - ln \underline{V}_t$ is the estimated proportionate future change in economic well-being, and the $\Delta ln(\underline{\underline{d}}\underline{V}_{t+1})$ $= ln(\partial ln \underline{V}_{t+1}/\partial A_{t+1}) - ln(\partial \underline{V}_t/\partial A_t)$ is the estimated proportionate future change in how wealth affects economic well-being. Finally, $\kappa_{t+1} \equiv r_{n,t+1} - \rho$ is how the market interest rate differs from the worker's subjective discount rate of future economic payments.

In our second stage of estimation, we also use an instrumental variables estimator, where we permit the degree of variability of the random error to differ across workers and correct the standard errors of the coefficients describing long-run preferences for the fact that short-run preferences have been evaluated using coefficients we have had to estimate. The variables we take as underlying the decisions producing the economic outcomes codetermined with labor supply in stage two include an indicator for each year, gross and net reported wages, the net three-month Treasury bill interest rate, children, age, age^2, (age∗education), health status, and home ownership from both three and four years prior plus net wealth of four years prior.

Labor Supply and Economic Welfare Gains

To examine changes in economic well-being from tax reform, we use the estimated short-run preferences from the first-step labor supply equation (A–1). Fully dynamic simulations using both short-run and long-run preferences make the researcher specify the entire lifetime expectations process, which is beyond the goals of this volume. Our simulations are known as lifetime consistent and are directly comparable to Hausman's static or single-year simulations. We apply numerical methods to solve for the jointly determined economic outcomes of interest because we have a set of nonlinear equations that depend on the income tax schedule, which makes the marginal tax rate and financial assets codetermined with hours worked.

The system of nonlinear equations we solve describes labor supplied, wealth accumulation, the marginal tax rate, and total tax payments using specific algebraic and numerical forms that are

$$h_{it} = 27.831 W_{it}(1 - \tau_{it})$$

$$- 0.4941 A_{it-1} - 2.0278 A_{it} + X_{it}\gamma + \eta_i + \xi_{it}, \qquad \text{(A–6)}$$

$$A_{it} = (1 + r_t(1 - \tau_{it})) A_{it-1}$$

$$+ W_{it}(1 - \tau_{it}) h_{it} - C_{it} - T(I_{it}). \qquad \text{(A–7)}$$

$$\tau_{it} = [\Phi_{1it} - \Phi_{2it}]b(I_{it}) + \Phi_{2it}\tau_{uit}, \tag{A–8}$$

and
$$T(I_{it}) = \int \tau(I_{it}) \, dI_{it}. \tag{A–9}$$

C_{it} is consumption expenditure, and η_i is the estimated individualistic labor supply propensity. $T(I_{it})$ is an equation describing how total taxes paid depends on a person's income (I_i), which is found by integrating (infinitesimally summing) the various tax rates paid on each dollar of income in the curvilinear marginal tax-rate equation, $\tau(I_{it})$. The specific numerical coefficients in the labor supply equation (A–6) are our statistically best estimates of the general linear equation described in (A-1).

We solve the four equations (A–6) through (A–9) for their four outcomes simultaneously using the Newton algorithm. In applying the Newton algorithm to solve (A-6)–(A-9) for the economic outcomes they describe, we take 100 random draws with replacement for each of the 532 men from a normal distribution for the stochastic disturbance, ξ, that has a mean of 0 and a standard deviation of 458. The value of 458 is the estimated standard deviation of ξ_i in the first step, where we estimate labor supply as the linear equation in (A–1). The Newton algorithm numerically evaluates the slopes and changes in the slopes (first and second derivatives) at each iteration, which yields comparatively precise estimates of each of the four economic outcomes.

After examining the labor supply responses to random disturbances to understand the pattern of how changes in the economic environment influence work behavior, we then calculate two so-called exact measures to infer the welfare implications of recent income tax reforms in the United States. The equivalent variation measure of welfare change we calculate is a hypothetical payment that a typical prime-aged married male worker could make to the government using his pre–tax-reform wage and capital income that would leave his welfare unchanged after the tax reform. The equivalent variation measure maintains economic well-being at its post-reform level, which under joint progressive income taxation depends on the post-reform wage and pre- and post-reform assets and lets wage differences imply a change in worker well-being across tax regimes. Our alternative calculation is so-called welfare variation, which is the change in the economic well-being gained by working at the going wage, also known as workers' surplus. The welfare variation measure holds the set of wages at the pre–tax-reform level and implies how well-being differs when taxes change. The welfare variation measure of moving from one tax environment to another tax environment is the change in worker economic well-being net of the actual tax revenue extracted. Both measures of economic welfare that we calculate and present in table 7–1 give similar ordinal rankings under revenue-neutral tax changes.

Selected Readings

Apps, Patricia, and Ray Rees. 1997. "Collective Labor Supply and Household Production." *Journal of Political Economy* 105 (1): 178–90.

Auerbach, Alan J. 1985. "The Theory of Excess Burden and Optimal Taxation." In *Handbook of Public Economics*, vol. 1, edited by J. Auerbach and M. Feldstein. Amsterdam: North-Holland.

Blomquist, N. Soren. 1985. "Labor Supply in a Two-Period Model: The Effect of a Nonlinear Progressive Income Tax." *Review of Economic Studies* 52 (3): 515–24.

Bosworth, Barry, and Gary Burtless. 1992. "Effects of Tax Reform on Labor Supply, Investment, and Saving." *Journal of Economic Perspectives* 6 (1): 3–26.

Burtless, Gary, and Jerry Hausman. 1978. "The Effect of Taxation on Labor Supply: Evaluating the Gary Negative Income Tax Experiment." *Journal of Political Economy* 86 (6): 1103–30.

Chiappori, Pierre-Andre. 1997. "Introducing Household Production in Collective Models of Labor Supply." *Journal of Political Economy* 105 (1): 191–209.

Conway, Karen Smith, and Thomas J. Kniesner. 1994. "Estimating Labor Supply with Panel Data and Taxes." *Economics Letters* 44 (1): 27–33.

Economic Report of the President. 1982. Washington, D.C.: Superintendent of Documents, United States Government Printing Office (February).

Economic Report of the President. 1987. Washington, D.C.: Superintendent of Documents, United States Government Printing Office (January).

Feldstein, Martin. 1993. "Tax Rates and Human Behavior." *Wall Street Journal*, May 7.

Hall, Robert, and Alvin Rabushka. 1995. *The Flat Tax*, 2d ed. Stanford, Calif.: Hoover Institution Press.

Hausman, Jerry. 1981. "Labor Supply." In *How Taxes Affect Economic Behavior*, edited by H. Aaron and J. Pechman. Washington, D.C.: Brookings Institution.

_____. 1985. "Taxes and Labor Supply." In *Handbook of Public Economics I*, edited by A. J. Auerbach and M. Feldstein. Amsterdam: North-Holland.

MaCurdy, Thomas. 1992. "Work Disincentive Effects of Taxes: A Reexamination of Some Evidence." *American Economic Review* 82 (2): 243–49.

MaCurdy, Thomas E., David Green, and Harry Paarsch. 1990. "Assessing Empirical Approaches for Analyzing Taxes and Labor Supply." *Journal of Human Resources* 25 (3): 415–90.

Pencavel, John. 1986. "Labor Supply of Men." In *Handbook of Labor Economics I*, edited by O. Ashenfelter and R. Layard. Amsterdam: North-Holland.

Triest, Robert K. 1990. "The Effect of Income Taxation on Labor Supply in the United States." *Journal of Human Resources* 25 (3): 491–516.

U.S. Internal Revenue Service, *Statistics of Income, Individual Tax Returns*, annual.

Ziliak, James P., and Thomas J. Kniesner. 1997. "Estimating Life-Cycle Labor Supply Tax Effects." Working paper, Department of Economics, Indiana University, Bloomington (September).

About the Authors

THOMAS J. KNIESNER is professor of economics at Indiana University, Bloomington, where he teaches courses in labor and health economics. He is also a visiting research fellow in the Division of Health Services and Policy Research of Eli Lilly and Company and a visiting scholar at Harvard University's Center for Risk Analysis. Mr. Kniesner received his Ph.D. in economics from Ohio State University and has been on the faculty of the University of North Carolina at Chapel Hill's Department of Economics and a visiting professor at Duke University's Institute for Policy Studies. He served as the senior labor economist on the staff of President Reagan's Council of Economic Advisers.

JAMES P. ZILIAK is an assistant professor of economics at the University of Oregon, Eugene, where he teaches courses in econometrics and labor economics. He is also a visiting assistant professor of economics at the University of Michigan, Ann Arbor. Mr. Ziliak received his Ph.D. in economics from Indiana University, Bloomington.